mobile working

changing the landscape

for future business

consultant editor:	Marc Beishon
managing editor:	Tom Nash
sub-editor	Lesley Malachowski
production manager:	Lisa Robertson
design:	Halo Design
group editor:	Richard Cree
head of commercial relations:	Nicola Morris
chief operating officer:	Andrew Main Wilson
chairman:	Miles Templeman

Published for the Institute of Directors and Vodafone
by Director Publications Ltd
116 Pall Mall London SW1Y 5ED
☏ 020 7766 8950 Ⓦ www.iod.com

Vodafone UK

Vodafone UK has 18.5 million customers and is part of the world's leading international mobile telecommunications group, offering a wide range of voice and data communications. The company is committed to providing mobile solutions that allow both consumer and business customers to make the most of now. In addition, Vodafone connects customers across the globe with roaming agreements worldwide. It provides 3G roaming in 29 countries and offers great roaming value with Vodafone Passport.

The Vodafone UK Enterprise Business Unit, the sponsoring body for this guide, is a dedicated division within Vodafone UK created to understand and satisfy the total mobility needs of all companies, from small business start-ups to large corporations. Its focus is to deliver professional services and mobility solutions that improve productivity, integrate with existing IT infrastructures and solve specific business problems.

For more information, please visit www.vodafone.co.uk.

CONTENTS

This Guide has been written by business and technology writers Marc Beishon, Nick Booth, Paul Bray, Piers Ford, Philip Hunter, Huw Morgan and Malcolm Wheatley

mobile take-off

**Miles Templeman, Director General
Institute of Directors**

One of the defining technologies of the 21st century is 'electronic mobility'. The 19th and 20th centuries gave us increasing 'physical mobility' through the ship, the train, the car and the aircraft. Those new freedoms transformed business and personal life, as well as facilitating very large-scale economic development. Electronic mobility gives us the complementary opportunity of being able to work (or play) as we choose, at any time and anywhere. The growing capabilities of wireless technologies will ultimately lead to there being no need to be physically tethered to communications or worried about batteries running down, whether in the office, at home, or on the move.

Such technical power represents a double-edged sword. Used well it can facilitate more fulfilling and productive business and personal lives. It offers new scope for improving customer service and responsiveness and many new opportunities to gain competitive advantage. But used badly, it could be a nightmare of poor practice, increased stress and uncontrolled costs. In particular, failing to follow good practice on security could snatch business defeat from the jaws of victory.

This Director's Guide is timely – mobile data applications are really taking off. According to figures from the GSM Association, globally the number of users of mobile broadband have risen tenfold in little more than a year, from three million in March 2007 to 32 million in April 2008. Mobile operators and service providers are bringing genuine business applications, and not simply technology, to the market. These applications, and the measurable business benefits that they bring, are particularly relevant for small and medium-sized businesses.

This guide outlines the new possibilities opened up by the tools of mobile working. It explains, in straightforward terms, the range of mobile communications options and gives clear guidance on establishing good corporate policies.

Stay on top of work when you're out and about with mobile email

Work doesn't need to stop when you're on the go. Get back to customers quicker with email on your mobile, from Vodafone. Available on a wide range of new and existing handsets. Stay in the loop, visit us in-store today, or call 08080 101 221.

Make the most of now

putting customers first

Elaine Roberts, Director of Enterprise Marketing, Vodafone UK

Writing this foreword it struck me that many of the business issues raised are fundamentally similar to those that we discussed in the previous Vodafone-sponsored guide in 2005: how to create a mobile strategy, how to successfully mobilise field workers, how to set company mobile working policies, and so on.

What I believe has evolved quite distinctly, however, is Vodafone UK's ability to meet the full gamut of those requirements.

Some years ago, I think it is fair to say that mobile network operators were caught up in a straight technology race, building the fastest and most technologically advanced products, with less consideration for the needs of the businesses that bought them.

Today, in 2008, Vodafone is focused directly on the customer. While we remain committed to delivering the highest quality mobile network, we have also attained a far greater depth of knowledge in the mobilisation of key IT applications, such as field force automation and customer relationship management. The result is that our new vastly improved 'mobile broadband' speeds are complemented by a sophisticated suite of professional services that are able to guide businesses on their mobile working journey and bring to life the dream of true flexible working.

One other thing that has changed in the last three years is the emergence of a new set of political and social drivers, including the 'green' imperative and the arrival of a new, techno-savvy generation in the workplace that many believe could change working structures and practices forever.

These issues are tackled admirably from a practical management perspective in this guide. They are also the subject of Vodafone's own ongoing Working Nation research programme (once you have finished reading this guide I also urge you to visit the Working Nation website at www.vodafone.co.uk/working_nation). Working Nation is a clear illustration that while mobility is what we at Vodafone live and breathe, we also recognise that technology always needs to be considered in the context of a working world and culture that is changing at a faster rate than perhaps it ever has before.

My sincere hope is that this IoD guide and the other research that we conduct at Vodafone will be of use to any business that wants to react to this change and adapt.

setting the scene

Marc Beishon, independent IT and business writer, outlines how mobile communications are changing the way we do business, and highlights the productivity gains and cost efficiencies already enjoyed by early adopters

Today, the mobile phone is such a ubiquitous part of personal and business life it is hard for even many older people to recall a time when instant mobile communications was enjoyed only by specialist sectors such as the police, armed forces and taxi firms. But there has been a long period where the main increase in use has been towards a saturation in mobiles for basic voice communications, with everyone wanting a handset having one – and sometimes several. As for the use of data and messaging over cellular and other wireless networks, the growth has been mainly piecemeal.

However, now the market is primed for a major step change in how mobile technology will integrate with businesses, and also with personal life at home and on the move. Key drivers are:

EXECUTIVE SUMMARY

☐ by 2011, more than 30 per cent of the worldwide working population will be relying on mobile communications to do their job

☐ meanwhile, the current lack of access to email while on the move is costing UK business more than £7bn a year

☐ mid-sized companies need to play catch up, as large and small companies take the lead in using mobile applications

☐ introducing mobile and flexible working will present companies with challenges around new working practices and processes

☐ changes in lifestyle, climate and regulation are demanding mobility for an increasing number of workers. There is growing pressure to implement flexible working policies and to use mobile technologies

☐ the demand by consumers for multimedia messaging services, social networking, transfer of large files, mobile TV and convenient payment services. In some parts of the world, mobile phone credits are enabling people with no banking facilities to carry out electronic transactions

☐ the demands by business for office applications and industry-specific systems that will work seamlessly in a mobile context, to keep pace with the increasing number of people working remotely, at home or on the move

In turn, it is new technology that is providing the backbone for these demands. The main factors are:

☐ the roll out of third generation (3G) mobile networks that can power much faster and more sophisticated data and messaging applications – true 'mobile broadband'

☐ the introduction of sophisticated handsets – including smartphones and personal digital assistants – that can use 3G networks, as well as devices that plug into laptop and notebook computers that also connect them to mobile broadband

☐ the development of a wide range of systems and applications that take advantage of 3G networks, such as unified messaging, where a handset can receive the same calls, messages and media as via a desktop PC and fixed line phone. These appeal to both consumers and business users

quantifying the demand

According to analyst firm IDC, the growth in adoption of mobile enterprise applications will match the growth of the worldwide mobile worker population. As it reports, there were about 760 million mobile workers in 2006, which will rise to one billion by 2011 – more than 30 per cent of the total workforce. In the US, more than 70 per cent of workers will have some level of mobility by 2011, while in Western Europe, we will see more than half of the workforce on the move as part of their jobs.

A key trend is the rapidly rising use of mobile information and data services. By 2013, 38 per cent of mobile phone users in Western Europe will use mobile internet services, according to analyst Forrester Research. This means 125 million Europeans will access the internet – browsing websites, for example – regularly from their mobile handset. This is triple the number that do so today. A key driver is the proliferation of 3G mobile devices, which will overtake the number of previous generation phones by 2010.

Forrester, which looked at trends across 17 European countries, also reports that the UK is among the leaders in 3G adoption, along with Austria, Italy and the Nordics. More than 60 per cent of mobile phone users in these countries will have a 3G handset by the end of 2010.

As a guide to the speed of adoption of mobile broadband services, it has taken just nine months during 2007-8 for UK connections to balloon from 30,000 to 125,000. And, this is using the freedom of mobile phone networks and not the localised Wi-Fi links available at 'hotspots' in places such as train stations and coffee shops. Shipments of low-cost 3G modems for notebook computers are booming, especially in Europe, as mobile operators set aggressive pricing plans for data services.

business trends

The clear leaders among users of currently 'rolled out' mobile applications are companies that are running systems for mobile field workers that carry out routine tasks. Applications such as job scheduling by location, inventory and order management, proof of delivery and so on, are in widespread use. These have migrated from specialised radio systems to the mobile phone networks.

Utilities, logistics and courier companies are the early adopters and leaders in implementing sophisticated field worker applications, where real-time reporting is often the most critical factor. Applications for professionals such as salespeople and financial advisers, where placing orders and checking customer data in real time is also important, are also a strong growth area.

So far, mobile office applications for professionals such as 'knowledge workers' – company executives, lawyers, healthcare workers, journalists, etc. – are not as widely deployed, but are likely to catch up rapidly. According to research from Vodafone, mobile email in particular is becoming an application that is critical to business performance. The research finds that:

- one in 10 businesses now expect a 30-minute turnaround on new business emails

- one in three businesses still expect a response within two hours

- over a third – 36 per cent – of UK workers say lack of mobile email causes unnecessary stress and conflict in the workplace

The research also calculates the costs of a current lack of access to email on the move as being £7.345bn a year, with an average cost to a company of lost opportunities of nearly £19,000 a year. But 10 million BlackBerry email handsets have been shipped worldwide so far, so this is not an early adopter market now, but a mature application that most organisations should investigate.

Indeed, while there is a long way to go in building mobile capacity for Britain's organisations, the indication is that it is considered a key area for investment, even during the difficult economic times in 2008. Analyst firm Gartner has reported that the majority of medium to large European companies were planning to maintain their mobility budget at the level spent in 2007, or increase it by between five and 10 per cent, and some by as much as 20 per cent. Again, email is seen by Gartner as the key application.

mid-market companies lagging behind

The most active adopters of new mobile applications are large and small companies. Mid-market firms are more likely to have less IT support and capital than larger organisations. They also tend to be more conservative and less agile than smaller operations whose usage is often driven by business owners and young staff members who are eager to get their hands on the latest gadgets.

Indeed, smaller businesses have much to gain by using devices and services targeted more at the consumer market, notes the Yankee Group, a telecoms analyst. It reports that of all consumer technology solutions, blogs, 'wikis', smartphones, wireless-enabled laptops, instant messaging and online travel services have the greatest impact on small businesses, increasing productivity by 25 per cent to 50 per cent for each mobile employee. On the other hand, basic voice-only mobile phones can actually decrease productivity, as can distractions such as YouTube (not surprisingly).

A trend for both business and home users is the ability to use one handset for all communications, which is where the new generation of smartphones really come into their own. Research by In-Stat has found that eight per cent of 'road warriors' in the US – ie. business people who travel frequently – have given up a desk phone to rely solely on their mobile number. But there is also a great deal of loyalty to tried-and-tested older technology and most users still prefer to work with multiple devices.

It will also be impossible to divorce people's personal use of mobile communications from their business use. Raw statistics show that more than 40 per cent of mobile traffic – over half of fixed-voice traffic – and the vast majority of broadband access traffic is now generated in the home. And it is probable that an increasing portion of this traffic will be work-related. Applications such as social networking are blurring the boundaries between work and personal life and are also driving mobile traffic. Consumers report that email and web browsing are key features they look for in mobile phones, although the ubiquitous text messaging and also the digital camera come out top.

A majority of people now take their mobile phone or BlackBerry on holiday with them and many will still be in regular contact with the office, by voice or email.

mobiles as an economic driver

It is worth noting that apart from productivity for individual companies, mobile networks have been measured as a major enabler of economic growth.

For example, research by Spectrum Value Partners shows that the European economy would receive a financial boost of at least €95bn over the next 20 years if one quarter of the UHF television band were allocated for mobile broadband services. This is in addition to the €2.5trn generated by the European mobile industry using other spectrums in the same period.

Freeing up more capacity for mobile broadband will create low cost services for people on the move across Europe. It will also promote growth in the use of mobile browsing, email and video services. According to Spectrum Value Partners, the move will also stimulate jobs and innovation in new companies as entrepreneurs respond to the demand for so called 'Web 2.0' wireless services, such as video sharing, social networking and online business applications.

Meanwhile the mobile industry itself is investing heavily in yet more evolution to even higher speed new networks capable of supporting advanced data and multimedia services. By 2009, capital expenditure by the industry on data services will surpass that for voice, reports analyst ABI Research. And, by 2013, the percentage split will be 67 per cent for data, 28 per cent for voice and five per cent for mobile TV.

future challenges

While many enablers are falling into place for the widespread adoption of sophisticated mobile services, there are challenges ahead. In particular, the introduction of mobile and flexible working can create a complex mix of new business processes and ways of working, and management and security issues.

The wider issues of flexible working are crucial to the mobile theme. Policies and training for users can be vital, but are often overlooked in the rush to roll out new technologies. Demand by employees to use the latest gadgets, and social networking and multimedia services, will place pressure on containing uncontrolled systems. Marketing to consumers and business people will increasingly involve a mobile element. All applications need careful planning and the right partners to be effective. These issues and others are addressed in depth in the other chapters in this guide.

HEADLINE MESSAGES

○ events in society – such as escalating fuel costs, the green agenda and demands for flexible working – are accelerating the need to investigate and implement mobile applications beyond basic voice

○ key enablers – including high-speed 3G networks and sophisticated devices such as smartphones – are available now at low cost

○ general mobile office applications are lagging field operations systems such as job scheduling. However, they will catch up rapidly in the next few years. Mobile email is an entry level 'killer' office and personal application for many

○ mobile systems can also play vital roles in activities such as business continuity planning and personal security

○ implementing company-wide mobile applications is a task that can require a considerable degree of decision making about technologies and management of concerns such as security. Many companies start with departmental systems as proving grounds. Development partners need to be selected with care

○ even analysts have a hard time predicting what people will find to be the most attractive major applications for faster and more sophisticated mobile networks. It is important to focus on what is practical and available now

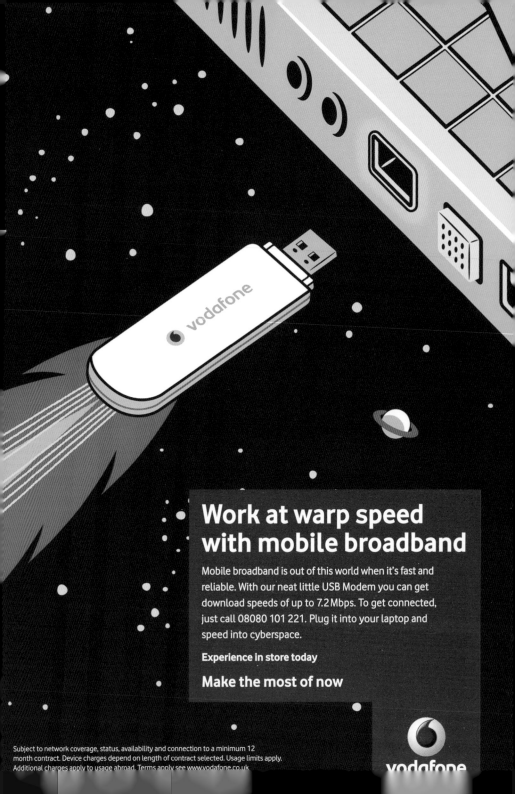

the mobile enterprise

Philip Hunter, independent business and technology writer, highlights how mobile technologies are enabling companies to meet new social and competitive drivers

What is the mobile enterprise and what factors are making it possible?

In just two decades mobile communications has progressed from being an expensive and unwieldy executive toy to the brink of delivering truly 'agile' working.

Recent advances both in the technology itself and in associated software services, such as unified messaging and diary synchronisation, mean that just about all office productivity applications can now be fully mobilised. For the large enterprise, these key office applications and other industry-specific systems have been mobilised for some time, but the same benefits can now be enjoyed by SMEs.

EXECUTIVE SUMMARY

- ☐ mobile office and industry-specific applications are now in the reach of companies of all sizes

- ☐ mobile services also provide the added dimensions of location, ubiquity and staff availability, which can greatly increase performance

- ☐ by fully mobilising applications, companies can also reduce their exposure to risk from events beyond their control

- ☐ mobile devices are becoming a key aid to monitoring staff safety and triggering alarms when personnel are placed in danger

Yet mobilising existing applications is just the beginning. Mobile technology by its very nature provides an extra dimension, with its potential to exploit location for tracking and monitoring of vehicles, products and employees. Mobile operators already offer a range of business and consumer services that exploit location for a variety of applications relating to productivity, cost saving, personal safety and environmental monitoring.

The fundamental step forward that makes all this possible is ubiquitous mobile access – to the internet, messaging, voice and even video from laptop computers and smartphones such as the BlackBerry – and also the use of various dedicated devices for tracking and monitoring applications. The combination of office and remote tracking mobilisation brings about the scope for the mobile enterprise in the following five categories:

- serving customers in a global market
- flexible working
- reducing office costs
- business continuity
- corporate responsibility

These groups overlap to some extent, with flexible working cutting office costs as well as boosting business continuity. This was shown dramatically at Vodafone during the wet summer of 2007, when the company's headquarters near Newbury were flooded. The billing department was badly affected, but fortunately, six months earlier all billing staff had been issued with laptops that replaced their desktop PCs. As a result, the department was able to keep working as normal via mobile communications and there was no disruption to customer service or support as a result of the flooding.

serving customers

In the first category the key requirement is the capability to communicate with customers at all times wherever you and they are, which follows from having near permanent access to the internet.

Sales representatives on the road, for example, have been mobile for years but were first reliant on public call boxes and then basic voice mobiles and were often uncontactable for considerable periods. Now orders can be placed, diaries checked immediately, customer data updated and retrieved, documents shared, and conference calls placed with experts and colleagues. Similarly, field service engineers can be contacted quickly and dispatched to jobs much more efficiently on the basis of their location obtained from their mobile handset. Meanwhile, parts information can be accessed and updated in real time. The availability of satellite navigation enhances such applications, especially when combined with real-time feedback about traffic conditions or the status of public transport services.

The possession of a mobile device can now also confer a 'presence' to others, allowing anyone to set preferences on how you can be reached immediately – by voice, text or email. Mobile email is becoming a particularly crucial application (see box on page 23 for results of recent research).

The recent arrival of broadband mobile services worthy of the name has also made a big difference. These allow high-speed browsing of websites and transfer of large files, such as high resolution images or video clips that are transmitted from and between devices. Operators such as Vodafone now support download speeds up to 7.2 Mbps and uplink speeds up to 1.44 Mbps. This is about 30 times the speed of early third generation mobile services, which not surprisingly failed to gain much traction. These higher speeds also bring the potential for attaching gadgets such as professional digital cameras to laptop computers for capturing and transmitting images from the field. Mobile phones are even being used for onsite medical diagnosis, via devices for capturing images.

While standard office applications are straightforward to implement, mobile systems tailored to some company-specific business processes will require adaptation of components from suppliers, and a good relationship with a development partner. (See chapters 6 and 7 for more.)

flexible working and office costs

The main focus of the second benefit category – flexible working – is on staff happiness and morale. The motives are not purely altruistic, for it is now widely recognised that happier staff are more productive and less likely to leave. A recent study found that the single act of allowing staff to work from home once a week reduced both absenteeism and churn significantly. (See chapter 3 for the latest thinking on flexible working.)

This leads neatly onto the third benefit category – saving office costs – with the main emphasis on hot desking. This can only be achieved in any case by flexible working, which reduces the staff to seat ratio. In this case the potential for savings is obvious enough, but even so, the extent sometimes surprises resource managers. Vodafone, for example, has implemented hot desking in a big way, with only half as many seats as there are employees. This 50 per cent level of hot desking has saved the company £7,500 per employee, per year.

Naturally, there is more scope for hot desking among larger enterprises, but even SMEs can exploit flexible working. For example, a growing business can avoid having to move into larger premises to take on additional staff, by progressing gradually to effective hot desking – almost by default. Mobile communications also make it easier to make use of contract or freelance staff, who will have their own desks.

business continuity

The fourth category – business continuity – is also derived from flexible working. Giving staff laptops, or even portable devices – with the facility to work remotely – whether over fixed or mobile communication links, helps to reduce exposure to disasters at the central office, such as the Vodafone flood.

Mobile communications also brings the potential to recreate an office at short notice in new premises in the event of such disasters. The underlying principle again is that corporate applications should be fully mobilised, providing the same functions whether they are accessed from an office PC, or remotely via, say, a BlackBerry. (See chapter 8 for more on business continuity.)

This raises another point, which is that staff should be given the mobile device best suited to their needs. A journalist or consultant needs a laptop to write articles or reports on the move, as well as a mobile phone, while a merchant banker may manage quite nicely with just a BlackBerry for all functions. But there is, in any case, the potential now to consolidate the devices employees need to carry. The latest BlackBerry Bold, for example, can function as a GSM modem when attached to a laptop, eliminating the need to carry a separate modem card.

corporate responsibility

The BlackBerry is also an ideal device for obtaining many of the benefits in the fifth category, relating to corporate responsibility. This is a large and constantly expanding field, covering responsibilities both to staff and the larger community, with the latter including environmental issues. Flexible working plays its part here by reducing the amount of commuting and travel to conferences, with obvious cost savings as well as environmental benefits, especially with the recent high fuel prices. For permanent staff, the cost savings from reduced travel go into the pockets of employees, hopefully offsetting the increased fuel costs and reducing pressure for pay rises.

But the aspect of corporate responsibility that is of particular interest to mobile operators is personal safety. This exploits recent developments that enable the mobile phone, PDA or other smaller dedicated devices, to monitor the safety of staff and trigger alarms when necessary. Staff are likely to be most at risk when on the move, with a significant danger of physical or at least verbal assault in many job categories, for a variety of reasons. Social workers or bailiffs, for example, are frequently assaulted when visiting clients, while bus drivers are at risk at their normal place of work, behind the wheel. Unlike CCTV cameras, mobile phones can obtain verbal evidence, and also trigger alarms.

In the case of staff at greatest risk, a standard handset may not be the most convenient device. With this in mind Vodafone has introduced a smaller dedicated unit called the Safeguard Badge. The badge looks just like the standard ID card holder that some employees already wear, so does not attract attention. It can record up to two hours of voice that can be relayed back automatically to a call centre. It has a set of three alarm buttons on the back that can be used to communicate different messages, with one perhaps for absolute emergencies.

This device is driven by Track & Assist software, which can be hosted or managed internally, with the central monitoring performed on a PC, and the mobile components able to run on mobile phones, PDAs and BlackBerrys, as well as the Safeguard device. It allows staff to send alarms or messages using the three buttons, which could trigger amber, green and red alerts. At the same time, the location of all staff can be tracked, with the obvious benefits for mobile workforce management.

Emerging legislation in a number of countries concerning employer responsibilities to staff is driving interest in such platforms. In the UK, recent changes in corporate manslaughter legislation mean that employers must now take all reasonable measures to protect staff working in vulnerable or dangerous situations.

It is no longer deemed adequate just to issue such staff with a mobile now that the technology is available for accurate tracking. The number of staff who are at least sometimes in such positions is substantial – perhaps as much as 25 per cent of the total workforce, although there are no accurate figures (and, clearly, there are widely varying levels of vulnerability).

cost control

Another quite different aspect of mobility lies in cost control. It is not much use achieving productivity gains through mobilisation if all the savings are thrown away on high data roaming charges, for example. In the early days of mobiles employers suddenly found themselves with high and unpredictable bills after having got their fixed-line voice costs under control. The same happened with the advent of mobile data, but now at last, with a little gentle encouragement from governments, mobile operators have got their prices under control.

It is now possible for SMEs to obtain quite modestly priced fixed-cost plans at, say, £50 to £100 per month per employee, covering their mobile voice and data requirements. This enables them to predict costs, and consolidate all communication services within a single bill. (See chapter 9 for more on mobile policies.)

the 'wow' factor

But perhaps the most important aspect of mobility – and one that companies may underestimate – lies in staff recruitment, motivation and retention. In industries where competition for the best staff is most intense, the availability of flexible working has become essential. Prospective employees will often ask for, or even insist on, some degree of flexible working during their interview, and can also be swayed by being promised the latest, coolest mobile devices. This is a point worth bearing in mind as a wave of new generation smartphones enters

THE MOBILE EMAIL IMPERATIVE

- ☐ 42 per cent of all workers now say they need to be able to access and respond to emails when away from the office during work hours, simply to keep the wheels of business turning. This figure includes 53 per cent of HR staff, 40 per cent of customer/client service professionals and 54 per cent of finance workers. (And, 30 per cent of all workers want email access when outside of usual working hours, rising to 40 per cent of middle management and 54 per cent of senior management)

- ☐ 58 per cent of employees believe that everyone will need mobile email access in the future. Twelve per cent believe that time has already come, while more than one in five employers believe the same

- ☐ more than a third (36 per cent) of the UK workforce is aware of occasions where the absence of mobile email access has caused unnecessary stress and conflict in the workplace. This figure rises to 48 per cent when relating to the London workforce, 60 per cent of sales and marketing professionals and two thirds of workers who spend (on average) half the week away from the office

- ☐ three out of ten workers suffer stress when encountering a very full inbox on returning from meetings. This rises to more than a third of younger workers, while 17 per cent feel anxious when they are 'offline'

- ☐ 35 per cent of the workforce also feel that the absence of mobile email access or availability leads to wasted time (such as in between meetings or travelling to events). The figure doubles among workers such as service engineers who spend some of their time outside of the office regularly

- ☐ the average time wasted across a typical working month equates to four working days a month – 31 hours a month (or a fifth of the working month)

Source: Vodafone, 2008

the market. These devices are 'cool' from a personal level, but they are also ideally suited for running many of the emerging location-based mobility applications, while also delivering core messaging and office functions. Indeed, we are now at a point where one of the biggest barriers to enterprise productivity – lack of interest in using tools that companies provide – is likely to be swept aside.

social and business drivers

Paul Bray, independent business and technology writer, outlines the key motivators for employers and staff to work flexibly

Most of us, it seems, are sold on the idea of flexible working – at least in theory. Time pressure, whether perceived or actual, is a major influence on people's desire to work flexibly. Parents and carers often need flexibility to juggle the school run or hospital appointment for granny. Meanwhile, people with no caring commitments also value highly saving time (and money) on commuting so that they can spend it on other things, such as leisure, hobbies, education, or even a parallel career.

In the first half of this chapter, we will identify some of the key social drivers for flexible and mobile working, before moving our attention to the key business drivers.

EXECUTIVE SUMMARY

- many people are willing to forego a pay rise in return for flexible working, which once secured can boost staff morale and productivity

- younger recruits do not recognise the confines of a traditional 9-5 day in a fixed-location office, having grown up using technology that enables them to communicate with anyone, anywhere

- since 2000, BT has saved £500m in office costs by introducing flexible working policies

- companies must find ways to meet the demands of customers who expect a round-the-clock response

In a survey for communications company Avaya, 92 per cent of UK workers said they would find it attractive to work for a company that offered flexible working, and 78 per cent said they would consider changing jobs for the chance to work flexibly.

Meanwhile, according to a survey for Microsoft, 73 per cent of workers regard the ability to flexi-work as a deciding factor in choosing a new job. And, a third of workers told another survey that they would even forego a pay rise in return for the ability to work flexibly.

Flexible working appeals people of all age groups, although its value is different depending on their needs and responsibilities.

the young generation

Many young people want to work flexibly because they know they can and they don't see why they shouldn't. Most have grown up with mobile phones, the web, email, instant messaging, chat rooms and other technologies that let them get information on demand, anywhere, and share it with whom they like. They are also used to keeping in touch with – and even making – friends without constantly meeting face-to-face.

Having lived this way at home and university, they naturally expect to do so at work, and they have the skills and experience to make a success of it. They may visit a social networking site to answer a work-related query as readily as an older person would ask a colleague at the next desk. And, many young people have acquired an instinctive ability to multi-task.

Flexible working is one of the top priorities for new graduates, and employers that recruit graduate trainees are noticing a definite change in attitudes, with questions on flexible working, sabbaticals and corporate social responsibility cropping up regularly at interviews and careers fairs.

WHY PEOPLE WANT TO WORK FLEXIBLY

- ☐ time pressure, whether perceived or actual, is a major influence on people's desire to work flexibly

- ☐ psychological pressures may also play a part. Many people find that flexible working reduces stress, and some say they can concentrate better (and so do a better job) away from office distractions

- ☐ autonomy is the other common reason people seek to work flexibly. They want more control over how they manage their time and organise their work, together with the freedom to make their own decisions and the stimulation and variety that mobile and flexible working brings

WHO MAKES A GOOD FLEXIBLE WORKER?

Wanting to work flexibly is not always enough, since many people find out the hard way that they aren't really cut out for it. Business psychologist firm Pearn Kandola conducted research on the personality types most likely to benefit from flexible working, and the results were in many respects surprising.

Openness to new experiences is a good predictor of success, so 'conservative' people who like routine and dislike change are less likely to be good candidates.

More surprisingly, the researchers found that the most successful flexible workers were sociable and extrovert, not loners as one might expect. Remote working relies on good communication – with managers, colleagues, customers, etc. People who don't set up and use lines of communication soon lose touch, creating real problems for their managers.

The second surprise was how resilient flexible workers need to be. The technology doesn't always work properly, there's no-one to moan to if things go badly, people don't always understand what flexible working really means (this can include family and friends as well as colleagues), and so on.

Most people can be defined as rule-followers or rule-breakers. The researchers assumed that flexible workers would be rule-breakers and mavericks, able to wing it and think on their feet. In fact the opposite was true. Flexible workers must be able to follow company policies and procedures, even without a manager breathing down their necks. Paradoxically, it's the well-organised who are most successful at being flexible and intuitive.

Many young people are getting quite choosy about who they work for, refusing to join companies whose ethos they don't 'buy into'. Nor are they afraid to say if they don't like the way their current employer does things. The generation now at school may be even more insistent. In a survey for IT reseller Logicalis, two-thirds of 13-17-year-olds said the availability of technology would influence their choice of university, and four-fifths had already thought about work/life balance in later life. And according to Vodafone's Working Nation research, while 18 per cent of the workforce as a whole believes that technology will change the way that work is conducted entirely over the next five years, this rises to 31 per cent of 16-20 year olds.

parents and carers

Young people are not the only group seeking or demanding flexible working, however. The biggest growth in paid working in the 1990s was among mothers with young children, and the ageing of the population means that more people of working age are now also having to care for elderly relatives.

A report for The Work Foundation, Changing Demographics, found that the desire for flexible working was highest among those caring for older people, with parents of young children a close second and parents of school-age children third. Interestingly, while women were much more likely than men to want flexible and part-time working when their children were young, both sexes were equally keen when they had older children or older-care responsibilities.

The legal right to request flexible working for carers of adults and parents of children under six has generated further momentum.

older workers

A third demographic for whom flexible working is becoming attractive – and in some cases a necessity – is older workers.

As pension prospects dwindle, full retirement after the age of 60 or 65 is a luxury that many of us can no longer afford. According to the Avaya survey, 80 per cent of Britons would be more likely to work beyond retirement age if they could do so flexibly. Furthermore, an NOP survey for Help the Aged showed similar willingness to work part-time in retirement.

business drivers

There are as many business drivers for flexible working as there are companies doing it, but most can be boiled down to three necessities: keeping staff happy, saving money and remaining competitive.

employee expectations

Flexible working is popular, so encouraging it makes a company more attractive to work for, aiding both recruitment and retention. For example, at BT – a long-time pioneer of flexible working – more than 90 per cent of women return to work after taking maternity leave.

TOP TEN TIPS ON BEST PRACTICE

There are a number of key issues that companies need to factor in when implementing flexible and mobile working policies to ensure that the change proves to be beneficial to both employees and the bottom line:

1. flexible working shouldn't be introduced piecemeal. It needs proper planning and organisation, although it can be best to introduce it gradually

2. consult staff and managers and get them behind the idea. But don't raise unrealistic hopes – not everyone will be able to flexi-work

3. be prepared to change business processes, redesign jobs or re-allocate work, as is required. For example, you don't want staff carrying confidential information on laptops

4. make sure people are temperamentally suited to flexible working, and provide support and training for those who need it

5. be prepared to assess people's performance by output (what they achieve) not input (how long they spend achieving it). This sounds simple but isn't, so line managers will need help

6. make sure flexible workers have easy access to the people and information they need within the company

7. keep flexible workers in the loop. Invite them to meetings, ring them up, share the latest gossip. They shouldn't think, "I'm always the last to know!"

8. the ability to work any time, anywhere shouldn't mean working all the time, everywhere. Flexible working can cause as much stress and overwork as it alleviates

9. respect those who don't want to, or can't, work flexibly, and don't overload them with jobs the flexible workers used to do

10. don't sit back. Flexible workers need flexible employers, and the best flexible working programmes are constantly evolving

As regards recruitment, if people don't have to be in the office every day, an employer may be able to source personnel from a wider geographical area. It has also been found that staff who are trusted to work flexibly often have a better attitude towards their employer, as well as being less stressed and better able to do their job. And, absence rates can also be greatly reduced, as people who feel a bit under the weather can work at home, and a sudden domestic crisis – such as a sick child or exploding boiler – can be handled without the need to take an entire day off work.

THE GREEN MOVEMENT

According to smarter working specialists Work Wise UK, the UK has 25 million commuters, who are spending around 40 per cent longer in their cars, trains or buses than they did three years ago. Whatever the reasons – traffic congestion, people travelling further to find affordable housing, etc – reducing or staggering commuter journeys could have significant benefits for the environment. Using government figures, it has been calculated that if every SME in the UK let just one employee work at home one day a week, half a million tonnes of CO_2 would be saved every year.

Such environmental considerations are becoming important, not only for the growing number of organisations expressing concern about corporate social responsibility, but also for their staff and customers. Around a third of Britons now describe themselves as ethical consumers, so it is likely that they will also want to be ethical employees. Among young people the numbers are higher still.

Flexible working practices have a major part to play. A survey conducted by YouGov for networking company Cisco reported that, in order to support sustainable business practices, 53 per cent of people would be prepared to work remotely, 48 per cent would use videoconferencing or web conferencing to reduce travel, and 46 per cent would change their working hours to avoid the rush hour. Thirteen per cent would refuse to work for a company with no policy on sustainable business practice.

cost control

Combining flexible working with 'hot desking' (dispensing with personal desks in favour of shared areas for anyone who happens to be in the office) can save a lot of money. Some smaller firms have gone completely 'virtual', with everyone working from home, while large organisations such as the Office of Government Commerce have closed entire offices. BT, where 70 per cent of staff work flexibly and 13 per cent are home-based, has saved £500m in office costs since 2000.

Smaller firms may use the money saved on office costs to employ someone of higher calibre than they could otherwise have afforded. Others find they can grow more easily because flexible working means they are not constrained by finding space for extra people.

Other costs can also be achieved. A recent study by Coventry University Business School found that savings in travel expenses among companies adopting location-independent working ranged from 18 per cent to more than 40 per cent.

competitive advantage

There is a lot of evidence that flexible workers are more productive. People can concentrate better at home and the technology required to enable flexible working can itself also aid productivity.

Coventry Business School found that people only manage to do five hours' work in an eight-hour office day, but eight hours in the same time at home. And, if they only come into the office for a limited time they tend to get things done more quickly.

Flexible working can mean flexibility for the employer as well as its staff. It may be easier to get flexible workers to work outside normal business hours, or to use them in short bursts to cover peak demand.

Finally, flexible working is increasingly demanded by customers. Salespeople are expected to attend meetings with their laptops ready primed with the latest catalogues and prices, and able to take orders on the spot.

Consumers accustomed to the 24-hour economy expect a response in the evenings and at weekends. Being out of the office is no longer an excuse for not answering an email. According to Avaya's research, 73 per cent of Britons would be more likely to choose a business supplier that made its staff available outside normal working hours, and more than half would pay extra for the privilege.

marketing and commerce

Paul Bray advises on how to take advantage of the unique benefits of mobile marketing, and avoid practices that will turn customers off

Would you like to reach customers and prospects anywhere, any time, using a medium they rely on more than any other, and that grabs their attention instantly? Of course the answer is 'yes', but substitute 'annoy' for 'reach' and ask the question again. There, in a nutshell, you have the dream and the nightmare that is mobile marketing and mobile commerce.

EXECUTIVE SUMMARY

☐ research shows that SMS messages are more likely to be opened and read than emails or printed promotions

☐ people use their fixed-site PCs to surf the internet in depth, but on mobiles they 'snack' on the web for a few minutes at a time

☐ concern about the security of purchasing items by mobile is still high, but a range of secure payment options is now available

☐ recognising that there is a right way and right time to market via mobile is essential. Ill-timed bombardment will simply alienate potential clients

Mobile is the tiger cub of the commercial world: cute and playful today, but with the potential to become king of the jungle. Analyst firm Gartner estimates global spending on mobile advertising at just $2.7bn in 2008. Yet this will represent a 59 per cent increase over 2007, and the figure could more than quadruple to $12.8bn, by 2011. After that, who knows? Just think how far internet commerce has come in the last decade.

Mobile has some obvious advantages. People check their mobile devices more often than their email or 'snail' mailboxes, and they tend to act on mobile messages instantly, instead of filing them away to forget later. Some age groups – especially the young – are starting to use the internet more via mobiles than on PCs.

rapid response rates

Response rates can be significantly higher. According to media agency Kinetic Mobile, more than 90 per cent of marketing SMS messages (texts) are opened and read, compared with less than 20 per cent of email and 30 per cent of printed post. And if you include a link to a mobile website in a text message there is a good chance the recipient will click on it at once.

If interaction is one key benefit of mobile, the ability to know your customer is another. You can never be quite sure who is using an internet connection, but mobiles are unique to their owners. As long as you have their permission, you can build up profiles of people's preferences, where they go and when they contact you – whether by text, voice or via your mobile website. Then you can personalise future communications or alert your sales team every time a major customer gets in touch.

surfers and snackers

The way people use mobiles and the fixed internet is fundamentally different. While internet surfers browse and research in depth, mobile users 'snack' for a few minutes, during slack time – on the bus, before a meeting, during the ad break on TV – or when they want something pronto – a restaurant/filling station/heel bar.

While children and young adults are the most enthusiastic recipients of mobile marketing – and the most likely to participate in mobile campaigns, enjoy gimmicky promotions and take up mobile offers – well-heeled business people are more likely to have the sophisticated devices and unmetered access that enable them to use GPS location, view video footage or delve into a website. Evidence shows that people of any age can be attracted by the right product. Take, for example, the bingo promoter that has run a successful SMS promotion to the over-50s.

HOW TO DO IT

SMS (text messaging)

SMS is easy to use and good for low-bandwidth devices. It can include a mobile website address for further information. The sender incurs a charge per message, although there are big bulk discounts.

MMS (multimedia messaging)

This enables richer content, such as pictures or more text. But not all devices can receive it, and the user may be paying data charges to view it.

mobile internet websites

These are a useful adjunct to SMS marketing and almost essential for mobile selling. Content can be similar to a fixed website, but limited user time, smaller screens and different navigation tools mean look and feel must be completely redesigned for mobile.

QR (quick response) codes

These are a kind of mobile 'bar code' scanned by a phone's camera. They let you put a digital address on an advert, beer mat, business card, etc. so that the user can text to a short code, go to a website designed for mobile access or add you to their address book. Although still in its infancy here, these are already big in Japan.

voice

A phone is still a voice device, and 'click-to-call' buttons can be effective, especially for less techno-savvy users.

raising brand awareness

In theory, there is almost nothing that cannot be marketed by mobile. Amazon and eBay have mobile websites, and mobile has been used by car manufacturers and soft drinks makers, supermarkets and sports brands, estate agents and cinemas. So while people are unlikely to buy a car on their mobile or even research the market, it can be used to raise brand awareness, by sending a customer video clips or images of the maker's latest models to their mobile, enticing them into a dealership by offering a free car wash or reminding them that their MoT is due.

Coupons and offers can be effective in generating footfall to bricks-and-mortar businesses or, driving traffic to mobile or fixed websites. These can be time-targeted, and can't be lost or forgotten like a slip of paper. Points collection schemes – where customers text a code from a product to build up loyalty points – are another option.

TAKE THE MONEY

In some ways a mobile device is more secure than using the internet on a PC, since transactions can be verified against a particular subscriber. But many people remain reluctant to hand over credit card details on a mobile, either because of security fears or because it involves too much typing.

A neater alternative is a prearranged payment facility such as Paypal (now available for mobile) or Payforit (backed by the big five network operators), which offers a standardised user experience, guaranteed security and fewer buttons to press. It also helps if users can use existing access codes and passwords from fixed websites.

Small payments can sometimes be made via the user's phone bill, but network operators are wary of accepting large payments because of the credit risk, and the hassle of complying with financial services regulations.

In time mobile devices could be used to pay for a range of services from car parking to cash transfers. You can already pay the London Congestion Charge from your mobile, and Gartner predicts a three-fold increase in the number of mobile payment users worldwide by 2011.

Making actual purchases via mobile is even more embryonic than marketing. You won't sell many cars or holidays yet, although this may change over time (people said the same about the internet). Low-value items, such as CDs and T-shirts, and electronic goods, such as ring tones and tickets, are a surer bet today. Many people still have security concerns about purchasing via mobile, but these are expected to dwindle over time – again, just as happened with the web.

too much of a good thing

So much for the dream. But what of the nightmare: the risk of alienating customers through inappropriate use of mobile channels? The first rule is to get explicit permission to contact customers and prospects by mobile. As well as being common sense this is required by law, as is a simple mechanism for people to unsubscribe, such as texting a reply saying 'stop'.

The second rule is to be realistic about when and how often you contact people. Many people feel more aggrieved if pestered through their mobile than by email or post, because it's personal and immediate.

There are no rules of thumb about when or how often it's acceptable to contact people, as it depends on the individual or group. However, people will tolerate a higher level of contact if:

☐ it's interesting and relevant

☐ they get something of value, whether it's a discount coupon or some useful information, such as the latest test match score

The best time to contact people varies according to age and occupation. People may respond during working hours to business messages, but lunchtime or the evening commute can be ideal for consumer offers. Schoolchildren are likely to see messages around 3.30pm – and, if you're lucky, show them to their friends.

One thing is certain, however. If mobile marketing and commerce grow as predicted – and there's every likelihood that they will – businesses will have to work ever harder to deliver more of what customers want, and less of what they don't.

I WANT IT NOW

A Holy Grail of mobile marketing is location relevance, namely the ability to grab a potential customer just as they walk past your premises or alert them when they enter your area. The technology for this already exists. GPS is accurate to a few yards, and 'triangulation' (estimating a phone's location from the three nearest network cells) can place someone to within a couple of blocks in a city centre.

However, because of issues of privacy, and the safety of under-18s, the law only allows a user's location to be revealed if they specifically request this, eg. by using one of the 'find my nearest' services starting to be offered by retail chains and mobile portals. These are worth considering, especially for businesses that appeal to visitors, such as restaurants, cinemas, shops, estate agents, etc.

A simple form of do-it-yourself location-finding is to include different short codes on different advertising hoardings, so you know which one the person is looking at.

For businesses that want literally to pull people in off the street, or onto an exhibition stand, 'bluecasting' – broadcasting short-range messages using the Bluetooth system – is the hottest new activity.

Anecdotal reports suggest that bluecasting can achieve slightly higher response rates than SMS advertising, although the medium is still very young. And, whether people will relish being bombarded every few yards with messages saying, 'It's happy hour!' or 'Step inside now for 10 per cent off!', remains to be seen.

choosing the right technology

Huw Morgan, editor of Mobile Choice magazine, gives an overview of handsets, mobile broadband and network speeds, Wi-Fi and more

There's never been a better – or worse – time for your business to invest in mobile technology. The good news is that the technology is now so advanced and the handset choice so comprehensive that the perfect solution for your business is out there. The bad news is that you have so many choices and options to consider, a snap decision could prove costly.

However, like any sound business move, picking the right mobile solution is all in the planning and it's worth asking yourself a few simple questions before you make your next step. For example: is it essential that you can manage your email anywhere and anytime? Is regular mobile internet access a priority? Do you need sat-nav or the ability to download new applications? Does a laptop figure in your mobile plans? Or are you simply looking for a basic handset for calls and texts, which can take a few knocks and won't run out of power in a hurry?

If the latter scenario fits, your decision should be fairly straightforward. After all, there are many simple mobile phones out there that do the basics well. As

EXECUTIVE SUMMARY

- ☐ the latest mobile broadband technology is 10 times (or more) faster than 3G services

- ☐ while speed is often a priority, it is also worth checking what level of coverage is offered where your home and office are located, and in other places that you visit regularly

- ☐ the latest smartphones offer a wide choice of features and it is important to select the right device

- ☐ pricing plans for mobile data are now much more simple and affordable via a monthly fee

a general rule of thumb, Nokia handsets are simple to use, Samsung and LG offer stylish designs and a slim profile, Sony Ericsson handsets generally offer excellent battery life, and there's even a new breed of ultra-ruggedised handsets, such as the JCB Toughphone, which can withstand plenty of punishment.

However, if you're looking for a fast, clever, more powerful mobile device with a little more business acumen and a range of applications to keep you organised, you'll need to research a little deeper.

making technology simple

For most business users, the Holy Grail of mobile technology is the ability to manage email and access the internet on the move. Mobile handsets may have performed both of these tasks for many years, but it's only now that the connected mobile experience has really come of age. And the key factor here is speed.

Before 3G technology became readily available, accessing the internet on any mobile device, be it a phone or a laptop, was a slow and tiresome experience. The arrival of 3G enabled mobile internet speeds around eight times quicker than they had been on the 2.5G network and you could also stream files and data and view emails with attachments.

The latest evolution of 3G technology is HSDPA (often conveniently referred to as mobile broadband), which can be over 10 times faster than 3G. As a result, browsing the internet over a mobile network can now finally be compared favourably with accessing the internet using a fixed broadband connection.

For the record, HSDPA stands for High Speed Downlink Packet Access and the network speeds available to you will depend on the operator you are with and the HSDPA coverage it can offer.

In addition to HSDPA, which enables rapid downloads, some operators and handsets now also offer HSUPA technology, which stands for High Speed Uplink Packet Access and enables users to upload data, such as photos and videos, to the internet at high speed.

mobile broadband

The good news for business users is that you can enjoy the high-speed advantages of HSDPA mobile broadband and 3G on either a phone or a laptop, and the UK operators are now beginning to offer data plans that cover both.

If you're using an HSDPA or 3G-enabled phone, you can access the internet at high speed using your phone's web browser when within HSDPA or 3G coverage.

If you're using a laptop and want to stay online while on the move, you can still connect to the internet via a mobile broadband connection. However, to do so, you'll need a modem.

The very latest laptops come with a modem or data card built in. But, for the many that don't, you can still plug in a USB modem or dongle, or even use your HSDPA phone as a modem to connect your laptop wirelessly to the internet. Vodafone pioneered the USB dongle, which simply plugs into a USB slot on the side of the phone. However, each of the major operators now has a solution.

Wi-Fi

As most of you will be aware, even when you're not within HSDPA or 3G coverage, you can still access the internet wirelessly at high speed if your handset or laptop is Wi-Fi enabled and you're within range of a wireless hotspot. Many venues offer users Wi-Fi access free of charge while using their facilities, but the most common model is the paid subscription model. A number of UK operators now offer Wi-Fi coverage (from a selection of authorised hotspots) as part of their mobile broadband plans and offers.

mobile broadband coverage

Before choosing a mobile broadband deal, it's worth checking out the breadth of coverage your operator enables, because your phone or connected laptop is only as fast as the network coverage on offer.

Bear in mind that, when you move out of coverage range for HSDPA mobile broadband, you'll automatically pick up a 3G connection if available. Therefore, it's also worth investigating which operators offer the most comprehensive 3G network coverage.

For example, Vodafone's 3G network currently covers 80 per cent of the UK and has already been upgraded to offer 1.8 Mbps HSDPA coverage.

To improve network coverage, the UK operators are now teaming up to share 3G and HSDPA network resources – 3 has partnered with T-Mobile while Vodafone has teamed up with Orange to improve the 3G/HSDPA network coverage they can offer customers. The operators plan that this will become a reality in 2010.

why speed matters

HSDPA data speeds are measured in megabits per second (Mbps) and the higher the Mbps figure, the faster the connection. HSDPA dongles, phones and services will usually carry the maximum data speed in brackets; rising from 1.8 Mbps to 3.6 Mbps and with 7.2 Mbps currently being the fastest. Incidentally, 7.2 Mbps HSDPA can be up to 14 times faster than 3G (384 kbps).

However, these data speeds are subject to optimum network conditions and should be treated as a rough guide only. For a more accurate idea of the download speeds you can expect with different levels of HSDPA coverage, see the table below.

time to receive		mobile broadband 7.2 Mbps technology (typical speeds)	mobile broadband 1.8 Mbps technology (typical speeds)
20 minute video	(150 MB)	10 minutes	20 minutes
large presentation	(5 MB)	20 seconds	50 seconds
large photograph	(2 MB)	8 seconds	20 seconds
word document	(250 kB)	1 second	3 seconds

simpler pricing

Data plans can be confusing when operators structure pricing according to pages viewed or amount downloaded. Fortunately, most operators now offer mobile broadband data bundle deals for a set monthly fee. Better still, a few of the operators are now offering data bundle deals that cover internet access on your phone's browser and internet access on a laptop, using your phone as a modem.

so which handset to choose?

Business users looking for a more sophisticated mobile device capable of utilising the latest technology should consider a smartphone. In addition to offering a wealth of functionality, smartphones will also allow you to download new applications. Smartphones function like handheld computers and run on an operating system, the most common being Symbian, Windows Mobile, BlackBerry, Palm and – since the launch of the iPhone – Apple.

As we've established, HSDPA data speeds will considerably improve the email and web browsing experience on your mobile handset. However, there are whole host of other considerations before you make your decision.

business email

If your business has its own email server then you'll need a device that can interact with that. The advantage of server-based mail is it gets 'pushed' to your device automatically as soon as a new email arrives.

The other kind of email, often called 'personal' or POP email, is internet-based email (Tiscali, Gmail, etc.) and is available on most smartphones.

Many smartphones now let you set the device to collect personal email at regular intervals or you can choose pick up email when you choose. Others will also let you access more than one email account. Smartphones such as the BlackBerry,those that run Windows Mobile and those made by Palm and Nokia integrate well with business email servers and handle personal email too.

a QWERTY keyboard for email

If you write a lot of long emails, it's worth considering a handset with a full QWERTY keypad, with ready access to commonly used symbols such as the dot and '@'. There are a variety of options here. The most common option is the QWERTY thumbpad favoured by Research In Motion with the BlackBerry Curve and Bold ranges, and Nokia with its E71. However, you could also opt for a slide-out QWERTY keypad, a design trait commonly adopted by HTC, or there's the virtual QWERTY, which can be found on touchscreen devices such as the Apple iPhone.

managing attachments

Many smartphones include viewers for attachments. Look for built-in tools listed in the specifications, and also for add-on software such as PDF readers, a Picsel viewer or Quickoffice.

When it comes to creating documents on your smartphone, you need editing software. Windows Mobile 6.1 devices can include Office Mobile, which allows you to edit Word and Excel documents, although it's a little trickier to create them from scratch. Nokia's business smartphones now include Quickoffice, which is ideal for document editing and creation.

touchscreen devices

A big screen can be a major asset on a business phone because it's ideal for reading long emails, viewing attachments and browsing full web pages. The Apple iPhone is one such device and boasts the excellent Safari browser and lets you manipulate content with its intuitive touchscreen interface. Other touchscreen handsets in the iPhone mould include the Samsung Tocco, the HTC Touch range and the Sony Ericsson Xperia X1.

Touchscreen handsets are perfect for web browsing and multimedia activities such as viewing photos and watching videos, as well as viewing calendar, contacts and enterprise applications. Because touchscreen phones such as the iPhone, Touch and Tocco have no mechanical keys, the screen can dominate the entire phone fascia and display full web pages. Some users find the virtual keypads on large touchscreens a little fiddly, but the other advantages are obvious.

For example, a map application on a GPS-enabled handset render so much better and the detail is so much clearer on a large touchscreen display than on a smaller mobile screen and you can easily zoom in and pan around the map with your fingertips.

sat-nav and more

A map application together with a built-in GPS receiver is becoming conventional on today's top smartphones. Nokia has invested heavily in sat-nav and many of its phones come with GPS as standard. Other manufacturers offering satellite-ready handsets include Research In Motion, Samsung, HTC, Apple and Sony Ericsson. The latest navigation phones feature Assisted GPS, which uses the mobile network together with the phone's GPS receiver to give you a faster location fix.

Once your phone has picked up your current location, it can be used for navigation by car or on foot in most cities around the world and you can also find and locate thousands of points of interest, such as restaurants, hotels, bars, petrol stations, cash machines and car parks.

final considerations

There are a couple of other considerations to take on board before you make your final decision. Roaming is an issue if your business requires users to travel abroad regularly, and you should also consider your data roaming needs, as this can have serious price implications if you haven't considered a suitable plan that enables you to use the internet abroad at a reasonable rate. Meanwhile, international calling rates are another consideration if your business regularly calls abroad from the UK.

Ultimately, there's a lot to think about, but if you work out the mobile technology required for your business to prosper and develop, the perfect solution is out there.

rolling out mobile applications

Nick Booth, independent business and technology writer, looks at the disciplines required to successfully roll out a more complex mobile application

Rolling out a major new mobile application can be a challenge. Every company is like a snowflake, with a unique shape and quality. Given the fluidity of modern enterprises – with mergers, acquisitions and new projects all constantly contriving to modify the company structure – even the same firm isn't itself a few months down the line. So it's impossible to ever expect an off-the-shelf solution to business challenges that goes beyond, say, a basic mobile email system.

That means that any application may need a high degree of adaptation. Even if your company is starting afresh, and there is no legacy business process to integrate with the new mobile application, there is a need to design it around the ways that people are working in practice – and not what desk-bound staff may dictate.

Nonetheless, the disciplines involved in a roll out are the same, whether you are starting a new process or just adding a mobile data aspect to an existing office-based business system.

EXECUTIVE SUMMARY

- major mobile applications should reflect the way that people work on the move, and not be a mirror of existing internal processes

- today's savvy organisations require suppliers to show proof of concept, agreed service levels and good use of existing resources

- applications should be designed so that users are not bamboozled with too much information or too many options

- analytical tools that can provide concrete evidence of success are a vital part of the project

tale of two companies

This can be illustrated by contrasting two examples of mobile application roll-outs, by companies from different ends of the learning curve. One is Aspective, a company that is owned by Vodafone, and which specialises in mobile workforce applications. As you might expect of a company with 150 customer engagements, it has considerable experience of how to deal with any mobile challenge.

By contrast, we can also learn much from some of the mistakes, and occasional triumphs, of one of the early developers of mobile applications. This now defunct company, which shall be referred to as company X, carried out pioneering work for a large metropolitan authority a while ago.

First, though, let's focus on Aspective, which has identified four major pressures faced by project managers for any new mobile application:

- ○ first, they have to satisfy increasingly demanding service level agreements for the availability of the application

- ○ second, they need to optimise the use of existing assets and resources. Unlike company X, which persuaded its metropolitan authority to pay for a brand new mainframe computer (when a PC could have run the application at a fraction of the price), today's savvy service buyers are likely to demand maximum use from their existing systems infrastructure

- ○ third, just as external service level agreements will be vigilantly observed, so must the productivity of the mobile workforce be visibly improved. The modern enterprise is a much tighter ship than it would have been even a few years ago, and every unit of time and money needs to be profitably accounted for, as far as possible

- ○ finally, there's the challenge of compliance. In these litigious times you are increasingly likely to be held accountable for any mishaps to stakeholders in your organisation, whether they are customers, partners or your own workforce. Your company needs a mobile system that makes it fluid, strong and adaptable. Lack of regulation would simply mean it was 'all over the place'

electronic monitoring services

All of these four pressures were on Aspective when it was asked to provide a series of mobile application services to G4S Justice Services, which is the world's biggest provider of electronic monitoring services. Law authorities use G4S to carry out 24-hour monitoring of home curfews, for example. Since many prisoners these days are well-versed in their human rights, this creates a challenge for the mobile worker in carrying out their job to the letter of the law. It also illustrates the attention to detail required within a mobile system, if the business process is to avoid falling foul of compliance regulations.

Any shortfall either way could lead to a situation where the client (the curfewee) or the worker (the mobile monitor) could end up having a legal complaint against the service provider. To make the contract even more challenging, G4S is also responsible for response, violation and evidence presentation to governments and government agencies.

masking the complexities

When there is little margin for error like this, it helps if the work schedule is simplified. In the case of G4S, each field operative (monitoring officer) is required to make 10-20 calls per shift. Aspective simplified the work scheduling process so that officers would be allocated jobs based on their skills, location and resources. The new schedule also ensured that the age and sex of the 'client' were also taken into account, thereby helping to avoid expensive litigation. Another important dimension was to mask the complexity of the system from users. Finally, the application was tested and re-tested before being rolled out.

By contrast, when the application that company X developed for its police authority client first went live, the mobile workforce – of wheelclampers and removals drivers – was bamboozled by the complexity and range of options offered to them on their laptop computers. This caused a massive backlog of unhappy customers. Fortunately for the supplier, the customers (members of the public whose cars had been clamped or towed) were then unaware of their rights or the correct complaints procedure. Such negligence would be fatally expensive these days, however.

an innovation too far

The problems that company X experienced stemmed from having to create an entirely new application, with no experience to build on. However, these days customers such as the Home Office (a client of G4S) expect an application to be built to complement their existing systems. In response to such expectations, Aspective deployed the Viryanet 'service hub' software around existing databases belonging to the Home Office. All silos of information – such as customer relationship management systems, spreadsheets, time sheets and customer orders – needed to be integrated and fed into the mobile application.

It is also important to avoid being too ambitious. Do not get carried away trying to provide tonnes of information to the end user initially. They will be seeing information on a reduced sized screen, so in the final analysis the information must be as clear and unambiguous as possible.

customer expectations

The company X example illustrates the point about customer expectation. In the early days of mobile applications, it was easy to get carried away and oversell the benefits of mobile data. The original system sold to the police authority was a mock up. Only when the company had won the contract did it begin writing the application, from scratch. Luckily, company X was given plenty of time to rectify its problems.

Unrealistic customer expectation would create many more problems today. G4S was a much tougher customer to please, but much more realistic. It had more defined terms for service level agreements. And, it gave Aspective just two weeks to provide a proof of concept. This tactic helps clients to sort out who are the experienced suppliers and who are overly ambitious.

A two-week proof-of-concept challenge is a good way to test if your supplier has the clarity of vision and experience to deliver. Unlike some of the other companies tendering for the business, Aspective was also able to work alone, instead of having to form a partnership with another supplier. Its conduct instilled in its client the confidence that it could deliver a workable system on time and on budget.

proof of success

Meeting the challenge of service level agreements, end user expectations and regulatory compliance issues are one thing. But the most important issue is the bottom line. How do you make the workforce more productive? And how can you prove you have done so?

Before you start, study a typical day in the life of a field operator. Note how many visits they are making per day and examine the bottlenecks in the process:

☐ are the operatives, such as sales reps, being held up by a lack of information about their client that hampers their ability to make a sale?

☐ is ignorance sending them on pointless visits?

☐ is lack of information about their own company (such as stock availability, or deals that can be put together) delaying or jeopardising sales?

☐ could more client visits be arranged in a day if they were better co-ordinated?

☐ could more jobs have been completed if the right parts were immediately available?

All this information, collated pre- and post-system installation, gives you an idea about how much value could be created, or was created, by your mobile application.

Demonstrating the value created by a mobile application is simply a matter of calculating the price of each field operator's man hours, and the number of man hours saved, and the increasing number of sales. A before and after day-in-the-life (DILO) study can go into detail about values, such as jobs completed per day, mean time between fixes and total travel time.

analytic tools are vital

This is where analytical tools are vital to the success of your project. Aspective, for example, was able to demonstrate to G4S Justice Services that it has improved the number of visits made by its monitors, and could demonstrate faster response times to curfew violations.

Sometimes, the value comes from unlikely sources. One company found its engineers were carrying millions of pounds worth of stock in their vans for the rare occasion when they might need it. Analytical tools could free up those static assets before they suffered depreciation on a massive scale.

Finally, let's not forget that not everyone will want your mobile system to work. Company X's contract with its client was met with massive resistance from some users, despite the fact that it helped the authority maximise revenue. This was because the end users did not like change. It was not in their interests and there was no motive.

the role of champions

In rolling out any system, identify the good, well-respected mobile personnel who enjoy using technology and are held in high regard by their peer group. They will champion the service to the rest of the workforce, who will jealously try to work up to their standards. It's a lot easier to get users to adopt a system voluntarily.

KEY POINTS FOR A SUCCESSFUL ROLL OUT

- ☐ optimise existing IT assets – is new equipment really necessary?
- ☐ configure existing systems for mobile platforms
- ☐ avoid escalating training and support costs by using a web-based system
- ☐ don't neglect compliance issues relating to your own mobile workers
- ☐ study existing practices to identify bottlenecks
- ☐ quantify costs of bottlenecks to prove return on investment figures
- ☐ manage expectations and set realistic goals and service level agreements
- ☐ identify users who will champion your cause

vodafone

Stay on top of work when you're out of the office with mobile email

Business needn't stop when you're on the go. Respond to those all-important messages with email on your mobile, from Vodafone. Available on a wide range of new and existing handsets. Stay ahead of the game, visit us in-store today, or call 08080 101 223.

Make the most of now

applications
and suppliers

Marc Beishon looks at the different service and product providers that are forming the rich landscape of the mobile applications world

In a market that is rapidly taking shape, where the majority of organisations are yet to embark on fully fledged mobile applications, it is especially important to navigate the various classes of provider and product to come up with the best fit for your business.

The diagram over the page illustrates the 'journey' that many companies will undertake when implementing mobile applications and as they grow. Three characteristics common among companies that are adopting mobile working are a need to grow, a need to empower staff and the need to keep a close watch on costs. In the public sector growth may also be a factor in terms of servicing higher workloads, while cost pressures, efficiency and staff empowerment are all key motivators for mobile take-up.

EXECUTIVE SUMMARY

- [ ] the mobile communications industry has spawned an array of providers that companies can use to ensure they get the products and services best suited to their specific needs

- [ ] specialised applications providers can help companies with more complex needs such as integrating unified communications

- [ ] managed software and services are of particular appeal to SMEs as they can offer both the latest technologies and cost benefits

- [ ] SMEs are also the most inclined to take advantage of technologies that are already widely used in homes

The mobility journey often starts out from the initial ubiquity of the mobile phone used for voice calls and text messages, but then progresses in functionality – and complexity – to mobile email and devices such as smartphones and laptop

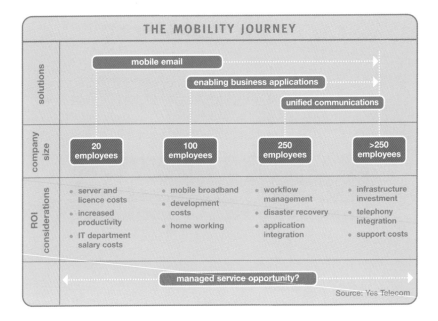

THE MOBILITY JOURNEY

Source: Yes Telecom

computers. These enable certain key business applications that can be used to great effect in the field. The next step is unified communications, which will help merge office and field applications with features such as single-number dialling for each person, and an online 'presence' for all members of a virtual team.

Kirona, a UK developer of mobile systems for the private and public sectors, also places the application journey in three generations:

☐ first generation – the 'dumb mobile' application. These are characterised by the download of data to a local device, mounted in a cradle, and have little real-time capability

☐ second generation – 'smarter application'. These offer real-time access capability to existing back office systems and mirror the back office system screens on a remote device

☐ third generation –'intelligent mobile'. The key is recognising that the remote worker 'environment' throws up different challenges, so reflecting the back office system design may not meet the challenges of mobile and flexible working

The reasoning is that a mobile workforce requires easy-to-use systems that are designed to work on the screens of standard handsets such as the BlackBerry, and which merge different applications to reflect the way people actually work in the field. For example, Kirona has a 'dashboard' module that drives access to systems such as job scheduling and calendar for each worker. As noted in chapter 1, this type of system is now in common use by both public and private sector organisations. (See also box on page 57 for a selection of applications and providers active in this 'field force' and other sectors, which demonstrates the spread of what's available in a very dynamic market.)

types of provider

A very wide range of companies now operate in the mobile application market, and it would be impossible to discuss them all here. But the main categories break down as follows.

operators

Major mobile network operators, such as Vodafone, not only offer systems, services and applications for all tiers of business, but also have partnerships with many other companies, including other operators and applications specialists. Some applications, such as business email, are available from the principal operators and through a large network of IT/telecoms business partners, while others are delivered by the application specialists.

While it can look like a complex picture, there is no denying that organisations have a wide choice of potential mobile partner. Yes Telecom, for example, is an operator partner for Vodafone. It alone has many business partners to deliver a portfolio of fixed and mobile phone services. These include mobile broadband, business email – including BlackBerry – and Nokia Intellisync, a product suite that allows desktop applications to be extended to mobile devices.

local IT partners

IT partners – also often called value-added resellers – are the firms most likely to engage locally with SMEs to install and implement all manner of systems. There

ECB: BOWLED OVER BY BUSINESS EFFICIENCIES

The England and Wales Cricket Board (ECB) manages the England team and promotes community cricket with event planning and support for school and recreational clubs. Many of its employees work remotely, and spend more than half of their day out of the office. They rely on laptops and the internet to check emails and scheduled appointments. But until recently, they found it difficult to keep up-to-date with new messages and changes to their calendar appointments throughout the day.

Chris Hoad, the ECB's Head of IT, says: "Employees had to wait until they found a connection before they could log on to their computers. It was easier for them to wait until they were home in the evening to catch up with emails. So our partners didn't receive fast responses to their messages and employees had to work long hours." Although some employees used BlackBerry handsets, these ran older versions of the software.

Hoad looked for a modern mobile solution to support ECB mobile staff. "I wanted to provide a mobile working service to all our employees, but my team didn't have the manpower or expertise to guarantee a seamless deployment," he says. After evaluating different devices with key users, Hoad decided to upgrade 70 users to the most recent version of BlackBerry software and devices. He contracted Vodafone Professional Services to lead a managed-device roll out, including training for IT support.

It took half a day to upgrade to the BlackBerry Enterprise Server, and three days to configure and activate all the devices. The entire roll out took less than two weeks, saving the IT team more than 70 hours of employee time.

All work teams can now respond to emails in real time, which helps them to make better use of their workday, says Hoad. For example, members of the account management team that support ECB sponsors can foster relationships more effectively now that they can answer email queries promptly, rather than waiting until the evening to send a reply.

And, the medical team carries a BlackBerry in its kit bag. If a player sustains an injury and needs urgent attention, doctors and medics can communicate with critical contacts and quickly check information – such as player medical history.

are thousands of these firms, but some specialise in mobile applications and have the requisite skills that cross the IT-telecoms boundary. For example, some specialise in applications such as Nokia Intellisync and Windows Mobile. Many that offer mobility as part of their portfolio are also able to offer ground-level business email and mobile broadband advice and implementation. Others may have strengths in wireless office networks.

Many companies have no need for specialist field worker applications but will want to investigate more sophisticated access to office email and other desktop systems such as those in the Microsoft portfolio. Chapter 5 details the technology choices at the handset level, and email such as Hotmail and Gmail is straightforward to access without any integration with office systems. Such integration requires that companies are running servers such as BlackBerry, Windows and GroupWise on their office networks. This leads to licensing, hardware and IT support costs that need to be factored in alongside device and service costs. But servers can also be hosted by managed service providers, offloading much of the support and cost overheads of in-house provision.

systems integrators

Systems integrators tend to focus on larger and more complex projects, although most local IT resellers offer some form of integration, such as with an office networks and business email. Companies such as Aspective are firmly in the high- value systems integration camp, offering a 'best of breed' portfolio for implementing, and consulting on, applications in areas such as field service and customer relationship management.

software and system providers

There are a huge variety of mobile software developers, which range from straightforward systems for implementing a scheduling system based on SMS texts, to very specialised field force applications for vertical markets such as healthcare. The ease of building complex mobile applications is now much greater thanks to what is termed 'mobile middleware', software tools that provide platforms for integration.

Another active class of provider is starting to specialise in unified communications, where office networks are switched to purely internet-type communications, allowing many new features that can be implemented in and outside the office, including internet telephony and fixed-mobile convergence, where staff can be given one handset and one number that reaches them whether they are at their desk or on the move. This is a big topic in its own right and mobility is one of its key parts. See also the recent Institute of Director's Pocket Book on unified communications (June 2008).

managed services

A category that cuts across these providers is the hosting of various parts of the mobile experience by managed service providers. Business email and SMS texting applications can be entirely hosted outside of an office network and accessed both from the office and from mobile devices. Similarly, more complex mobile applications can also be provided on a managed basis.

'Software as a service' is another class of application that, while not just aimed at mobile workers, is also hosted for all in a company. Leading exponents include Salesforce.com for customer relationship management. Another is Google, with its Google Apps suite that allows mobile access on phones such as the BlackBerry to email, calendar, instant messaging and also documents.

Managed services and software as a service are of particular interest to SMEs as they offer elimination of some capital costs, predictable spend and access to the latest technologies.

device makers

While devices such as mobile handsets are often provided as part of a contract they can also be bought separately. The major mobile phone makers such as Nokia and Sony Ericsson are great sources of information about the latest technology, and have extensive resources on their websites. But there are many other portable devices that can be investigated as part of a mobile set-up. These range from printers, specialised rugged terminals, phones and notebook computers to Bluetooth wireless gadgets, such as earphones, projectors and personal navigators.

consumer technology

As noted in chapter 1, many smaller businesses are well served by technologies that are widely used by people in their personal life. The home will also see the introduction of systems such as 'one number' handsets and other services that are also pitched at businesses such as remote backup. Meanwhile, social networking applications and those provided by big players such as Microsoft

MOBILE PLAYERS – APPLICATION AND SYSTEM SELECTION

- ☐ Aeromark – supplies mobile workforce and fleet management systems
- ☐ AirVersent – specialises in supply chain logistics, proof of delivery and field service
- ☐ Apresta – systems include field sales and service mobility
- ☐ Aspective/Vodafone – the Vodafone Applications Service mobilises enterprise applications such as Salesforce.com, Oracle, SAP and Siebel onto mobile devices
- ☐ Cognito – provider of managed mobile data services for field workforce management
- ☐ Dexterra – offers Concert, which mobilises existing business systems on popular devices
- ☐ GPSX – its Condor Explorer provides secure mobile access to office files that can be printed, viewed and emailed using a BlackBerry
- ☐ Impact Applications – mobile offerings include a managed service for social housing contracts
- ☐ Kirona – provides mobile application development for the public and private sectors
- ☐ Medify Solutions – develops the MedifyRemote application, which allows GPs or healthcare professionals to access, update, and review patient records via a PDA/smartphone
- ☐ Microlise – specialises in fleet and distribution
- ☐ PaperIQ – provides a digital pen and paper to connect existing paper processes to enterprise systems, supporting mobile devices such as the BlackBerry range
- ☐ Premiere Global – offers web and audio conferencing, email, SMS, fax, automated speech and other technologies
- ☐ TBS – its TaskMaster mobility solution enables organisations to communicate with field workers
- ☐ Telmap – provides mobile mapping and navigation
- ☐ Ubisys – implements digital pen and paper systems
- ☐ VSc Solutions – offers supply chain fulfilment software
- ☐ Wire-e – provides Rapide for voice and text broadcasts to company staff

and Google will be more than adequate for fulfilling the needs of agile young companies, many of which may well dispense altogether with conventional office space and working practices.

business continuity and security

Piers Ford, independent business and technology writer, gives advice on how planning for business continuity and protecting against threats to data loss on the move

Mobile communications can play a crucial role in preparing businesses for operational difficulties, but can also pose some security concerns.

EXECUTIVE SUMMARY

☐ a company that integrates mobile BCP into the development of its people and its practices will help protect against disruptions

☐ fears over lost laptops, PDAs, etc., and therefore data, can be partially alleviated by ensuring security policies are robust and up to date

☐ security policies include both technical and people dimensions – and the latter is crucial

☐ managing how – and what – data is accessed remotely is a key part of the mobile security picture

business continuity planning – a natural fit

Mobile communications is increasingly being recognised as the lynchpin of business continuity planning (BCP), which is rapidly emerging as a major concern for SMEs. As recent events such as the Buncefield oil depot fire of 2006 and the summer floods of 2007 confirm, mobile devices can minimise the impact of disruption to company systems, whether the data centre itself is unavailable or simply because key staff are unable to reach the office.

Those businesses – relatively few – that were able to switch essential core processes, including data access and communications systems, to a mobile network were able to restore and maintain at least a skeleton operation during the crises, even if they had not previously established a formal, tried-and-tested BCP strategy.

BEST PRACTICE STRATEGY

A mobile BCP strategy should:

- [ ] be an extension of the business's existing communications capability
- [ ] be manageable from any location
- [ ] include and describe any compliance or reporting features
- [ ] be reliable
- [ ] be secure and confidential

---

integral to ongoing development

Mobile BCP should now be integral to the ongoing development of a company's mobile staff and the tools that they use on a daily basis. If that is the case, when business is disrupted – and as long as staff fully understand their roles and responsibilities – they will make an easier transition to alternative practices when the continuity plan is invoked. But many directors remain unaware of the efficiency and flexibility benefits of mobile BCP, perhaps because of assumptions about the costs and complexities involved. However, they are aware of the potential consequences of disruption:

- estimates of the financial cost of disruption range from £10,000 an hour for a customer-facing SME, to millions of pounds for a large financial services company

- length of disruption is also a major issue. More than 30 per cent of directors asked by journal Continuity Central what the length of a potentially fatal disruption to their business would be – with at the very least, lack of access to key communications systems, customer support and financial systems – said that it would be less than four hours

However, half the SME directors canvassed for a Populus survey in the summer of 2007 – ironically just before the rains came – did not have a written BCP in place.

Although the situation is superficially brighter among larger businesses, with 81 per cent of mid-market companies having some kind of BCP, according to security specialist Activity, only 15 per cent have tested those plans thoroughly and are convinced they will work.

nurturing the right culture

Mobile is not a silver bullet. The success of any integrated BCP strategy will depend on the prevailing attitudes within the company's existing mobile culture. Its effectiveness as a defence is therefore limited to reflecting and exploiting the company's use and experience of mobile communications and data.

Reinforcing the mobile aspect of the framework and ensuring that staff are geared up to enact those policies need not be a complicated or expensive process. Nonetheless, it will almost certainly require a new focus on the training, attitudes and knowledge of the people who will be relying on mobile communications to fulfil their roles, if events dictate. It may also require a different focus on the tools they use. Key points include:

- successful BCP is about delivering critical services within a timeframe that's acceptable to the business – if the worst happens

- it demands a clear understanding of the minimum requirements for delivering those services – what they are, the enabling technology, and the people who access them

- many SMEs still tend to have a single-site data communications centre, rendering them more vulnerable to disruption. 'Software as a service' applications would give mobile users access to hosted systems via the internet, regardless of their location

- the next wave of hosted services – collaborative applications – would allow mobile users to continue working together even if the data centre was out of action

mobile security alert

Disasters aside, other events – particularly some very public examples of serious data loss – continue to expose lax end-user attitudes to mobile security, symptomatic of poorly conceived and enforced policy. These suggest that staff awareness of their mobile responsibilities could be a bigger issue than technical sophistication. If firms want their staff to take full advantage of the cost/flexibility benefits of mobile working, this is one area that needs close attention.

laptop loss fears

Scarcely a week goes by without a data loss headline, usually involving a mislaid or stolen laptop, or a missing CD that inevitably contains several thousand customer details. (Nowadays, it could just as easily be a smartphone or PDA.) Such incidents create fear – either of the penalties implied by the swelling tide of Data Protection legislation and compliance standards such as the Payment Card Industry's Data Security Standard, or simply of the damage to a business's reputation when such a basic security breach fractures customer trust. This is hardly the ideal climate in which to realise a mobile security strategy. Instead of living in fear of becoming the next headline, organisations should make the constant testing and reinforcement of solid policies a priority.

inconvenience and inefficiency

A lost laptop doesn't just constitute a security risk. Without it, the user can't work, and any data held on the laptop that hasn't been backed up centrally is also lost, possibly leading to delayed billing and payment. Consider that:

- 92 per cent of European SMEs with mobile workers have experienced laptop theft

- less than three per cent of SME laptops stolen are ever returned

- 58 per cent of the cost of each theft is tied up in the value of the data held on the laptop rather than the hardware itself

- compromised customer information security is a major concern for 37 per cent of European SMEs worried about laptop loss, and a high concern for another 38 per cent

- compromised employee information and general company information follow closely behind, with breaches of company, partner and customer networks and intranets also a serious worry

Research by Microsoft suggests that only 25 per cent of laptop users actually lock their mobile devices. A mobile security policy should cover even the most basic principles and so complement the firewall, encryption and device management technology deployed as the main defences against threat.

These principles should include:

O   regular awareness campaigns

O   training. In one survey, only 39 per cent of information security officers in the UK, US, Canada and China offered specific security training to mobile workers, although the number is rising

O   physical laptop security guidelines

O   enforced, frequent password changes, even down to USB flash drives or 'sticks' (there are now encrypted drives on the market that enforce strict password generation rules). You can also get memory stick and notebook computers with fingerprint verification

O   user data backup – manual and automated

O   data categorised according to sensitivity, with high-risk data classified as non-portable

O   user guidelines governing use and transportation

end-to-end data management

Mobile security and overall data management policies must of course be integrated. Giving the right people secure access to certain systems becomes even more important when they work remotely from the office, and is raising additional security concerns for IT managers. But there is also a need for balance, allowing some flexibility in the type of mobile device and ease in quickly getting staff running with new processes. If staff are allowed to use their own devices on the company network, applications could be restricted accordingly – perhaps to email – and the device configured to return to its default settings when the user leaves the company. (See also p64.)

Security policies should not focus entirely on laptops, either. Many firms now encourage their staff to use SMS and email on smartphones rather than voice to communicate, meaning that the handset itself is a potential data security risk:

O   58 per cent of respondents to a recent McAfee survey are concerned about the theft of data stored on their phone

MOBILE ACCESS THAT'S FIT FOR PURPOSE

Fitness First is one of the UK's most popular fitness chains, with 180 health clubs and 130 mobile staff in its sales, facilities and operational management team.

The company's staff use laptops to access emails and business applications but until recently, they were hampered by a range of challenges:

- the security risk of unsecured network connections meant that some strategic applications couldn't be accessed
- report and email applications were complex to open and download
- laptops had to be physically returned to IT support for repairs and upgrades, leaving staff without a primary business tool for the duration

As a result, internal and customer communications could be frustratingly slow, and while the laptops were a vital tool, they were also a security risk.

Fitness First implemented Vodafone's Secure Remote Access Solution in 2006. Employees now link automatically to the company network via a secure virtual private network (VPN) connection. A single icon highlights available internet connections and links them directly to their business applications. Staff now have access to the key customer retention reports and financial information which allow them to make instant business decisions.

"Employees no longer interrupt their busy schedules to bring laptops to us three times a year for updates. It's all done remotely, leaving them free to get on with their work," says David Glasbrook, IT services manager at Fitness First. "They have a reliable connection to email and other applications that's fast. This means they can respond to queries or organise their work faster and more efficiently.

"It is so simple that all our mobile workers want to use the solution."

- anti-theft software can alert users to any attempts to use their phone with an unauthorised SIM card

Organisations should ask their mobile service providers about the best combination of devices and security services for their protection needs. But opinion is divided over where the ultimate responsibility for security on mobile services should lie. In an Mformation Technologies survey of 200 chief information and telecoms directors from Global Fortune 500 organisations, 85 per cent felt that mobile operators should provide some mobile device management function, and 60 per cent said they were not happy with their current mobile service provider's management offering.

provisioning

Equipping mobile users is a vexed issue for IT managers. Apocryphal tales abound that the first sign of a disrupted company network is an irate call from the CEO demanding to know why their BlackBerry isn't working properly. End-users at every level tend to wear their 'consumer' rather than their 'business' hats when it comes to demands for the latest and best the market has to offer. Procurement, finance and IT heads, on the other hand, prefer to impose the devices on the workforce that best suit their budget.

Somewhere between lies the common ground where the right people – key staff and those who conduct most of their communications by email – have the leading edge, BlackBerry-type handsets that will be their principal communications tools in the event of business disruption. For others, a standard push-dial handset may be sufficient. Getting mobile workers to appreciate this in the context of BCP and security policies is one of the IT manager's greatest challenges.

policies for productive use

Malcolm Wheatley, independent business and technology writer, stresses the importance of having a clear policy on mobile communications usage

When employers provide mobile phones for use by employees, they often find it can be a two-edged sword. Used properly, an employer-provided mobile communications device – be it an ordinary mobile phone or BlackBerry-type device – can boost productivity, provide access to better and more 'business friendly' charging structures, and deliver higher levels of customer service. Used improperly, mobile devices can open the door to abuse, higher charges – and even brushes with the law.

Avoiding misuse can't be left to chance. However long-serving and diligent the employee, mobile communications is an area in which it is best to have clear policies in place, outlining how mobile devices should – and shouldn't – be used.

Over the top? Note the use of the phrase 'mobile device'. Yes, some users will see mobile communications as simply an extension of the phone on their office desk. For others, it will be the possibilities for data communications that will be the issue. For each, it's a requirement that should be met affordably, and in a

EXECUTIVE SUMMARY

- [ ] all employers need a policy statement that sets out clear do's and don'ts for their use of mobile devices

- [ ] employers need to decide how to handle non-business use of mobile devices to resolve both cost and tax issues

- [ ] the policy statement should include specific reference to preventing mobile devices from being used for illegal purposes

- [ ] data, as distinct from voice, communications poses serious cost, security and privacy risks, if not managed properly

manner consistent with individuals' roles and responsibilities. Those without a regular office desk, for example, do require both voice and data telephony.

making it clear

Every company needs to develop a policy statement that makes it clear how mobile communication devices should and shouldn't be used. Any employer that fails to put clear definitions in place – detailing precisely what counts as permissible use and what doesn't – is leaving itself unnecessarily exposed.

Should incidents of unacceptable use come to light – and a policy not be in place – employees can claim that 'they didn't know', or that 'they'd done it before, and no one objected'. A written policy statement removes that ambiguity.

To be effective, a mobile communications policy needs to:

☐ be written in clear and non-technical jargon. Mobile communication terminology can get complex, and employees can't be expected to obey rules that they don't understand

☐ contain examples of both appropriate and inappropriate use

☐ be sensitive to the range of roles and responsibilities within the business, and the legitimate variation that they place on mobile communications usage. There's no point, for example, in banning all data downloads and then sending the financial director a spreadsheet to look at while he or she is away on business

☐ be updated regularly. Today's mobile devices can do far more than those of ten or even five years ago, and usage policies need to reflect this

☐ be clear as to the nature – and amount – of personal, non-business use that is permissible

defining 'business use'

An employer provides – and pays for the use of – a mobile communications device because it enables the employee to work more effectively in the interests of the business. Otherwise, it's a 'perk', with all that this implies under UK tax law.

ATTITUDES AND BEHAVIOUR IN MOBILE WORKING

- [ ] one in four of us have used our work-issued laptops or mobile devices to watch online TV, and 10 per cent of men have used them to visit adult sites
- [ ] nearly 60 per cent of us consider our work-issued laptop or mobile device to be our own property
- [ ] one in three businesses do not have any clear policies outlining IT use for laptops or mobile devices outside of the office
- [ ] nearly a quarter of all businesses have experienced security issues as a result of employees using their laptops or mobile devices outside of work in contravention of company policy
- [ ] nearly half of us are not sure whether there are different policies when using IT inside/outside of work
- [ ] one third of workers either know they have company IT policies but have never read them, or are unsure if they have them or not and have consequently never read them if they do exist

Source: Vodafone UK 2008

But, as with deskbound landlines, some element of personal use is unavoidable, unless employees are to be rigidly required to restrict all such personal use to a separate – personal – phone. It's the purpose of the policy statement to set out what level of personal use is fair and appropriate, and what isn't.

Most employers would regard an employee calling home to explain that they have been delayed at a meeting or customer visit as fair and appropriate. Equally, most would regard a premium-rate vote for a celebrity on a television show as not fair or appropriate. While aiming to cover every potential example of fair and unfair use is unrealistic, a few well-chosen examples should make it possible for employees to work out for themselves the correct course of action in most circumstances.

Ideally, the policy should be clear on the use of business-supplied mobile phones by employees calling home when staying away on business. Obviously, such calls should be of a reasonable length. But equally, it's counter-productive to ban all such calls, and then see employees put through expense claims for more expensive – and permitted – calls made on higher-cost hotel room phones.

One solution is to freely allow personal use of a business-supplied mobile, but charge the personal usage back to the employee, perhaps via a monthly deduction at the payroll stage.

A number of mobile operators offer the facility to 'split bills' in this way, providing detailed records so that business and personal usage can be readily distinguished. Compared to the costs of operating their own mobile phone, it's even possible for this to work out cheaper for employees, as it allows them to benefit from corporate rates negotiated between employers and the mobile provider.

Finally, note that whatever the means used to distinguish personal use from business use, businesses cannot recover VAT for non-business use. When there is personal and business use of the same mobile device, then a 'fair and reasonable' apportionment should be made. VAT audits, it should be noted, specifically look for compliance with this requirement.

mobile communications and the law

Speaking of compliance, it's important that policy statements should make it clear that the use of business equipment for illegal purposes is prohibited. Once again, if that sounds extreme, it isn't. The best policies:

☐ specifically prohibit the downloading of inappropriate digital content, such as pornographic images, even if such content bypasses the filters that many mobile providers have in place

☐ specifically prohibit inappropriate or illegal calls to third parties, such as calls of a harassing or threatening nature

☐ specifically state the employer's expectations regarding the use of mobile communications devices while driving a vehicle. Under UK driving law it is a specific offence to hold and use a mobile phone or similar device when controlling a vehicle, and the policy statement should stress that employers expect employees to abide by the law. The only exception is when a driver has made a genuine emergency call to 999, in circumstances when he or she considered it would have been unsafe to pull over and stop

Hands-free kits of various descriptions are available, and these should be fitted to employees' vehicles if you consider it important that employees remain contactable while driving. However, remember that even if employees are using a hands-free car kit, they can still be prosecuted for offences such as dangerous driving if they fail to keep proper control of the vehicle they are driving.

Even so, to avoid increasing the risk of an accident, responsible mobile operators generally recommend that drivers pull over to take or make a call. A policy statement can reiterate this recommendation, and add words to the effect that:

☐ emotional or complex calls increase the risk of an accident

☐ the use of pre-programmed numbers helps to maintain driver concentration when initiating a call

☐ shorter calls are safer than long ones

☐ driving conditions can affect concentration and quality of decision-making during a call

cost containment

Employee behaviour – at management level and more generally within the organisation – can have a major impact on the costs of mobile communications. Any business wishing to make sure that its mobile communication costs are providing value for money will want to include points such as the following in the policy statement:

☐ it is the responsibility of the heads of named functions within the business (ideally IT or purchasing), to conduct periodic mobile communications spend analyses in order to ensure that costs, invoices, tariffs and spend levels are appropriate and not excessive

☐ it is the responsibility of all employees to make and receive mobile calls and digital transmissions over the lowest-cost device or network reasonably accessible to them. For example, this means using a landline or digital network rather than their wireless equivalents, when these are within ready reach

- employees with smartphones should always consider if a digital text-based email message will be cheaper than a voice call

- employees must act with due diligence when caring for mobile equipment in their custody. Employers will lay down (where considered appropriate) sanctions for loss, damage or misuse

- users must always endeavour to use a lower cost directory enquiry number or an internet enquiry service, where possible

- employees should note that spend analyses and other such monitoring systems and exercises are in place, and that the misuse of business-supplied mobile equipment for personal or other use will be identified

digital data and digital communications

Finally, in today's digital era it is important for any policy statement to make it clear how the business wants its employees to respond in respect of digital – as opposed to voice – communications.

In general, digital downloads are relatively expensive (especially, at present, outside UK borders). So, businesses will want to consider the extent to which they expose themselves to this expense, and the level of employee for whom it is considered appropriate, even supposing that the digital downloads in question are legitimate – in the form of company spreadsheets, presentations and suchlike.

However, there are other issues relating to digital data, principally revolving around security and privacy. Accepting for the sake of argument that mobile devices have a higher risk of theft than deskbound devices in the office, it is important for employees to make full use of the password protection their devices afford them. Otherwise, potentially sensitive information could fall into the hands of third parties.

And in the case of digital data relating to identifiable persons, the employee – and, through them, the employer – has a responsibility under UK and European data protection laws to exercise a duty of care over that data, to prevent its loss or subsequent misuse.

future opportunities

Philip Hunter offers a tantalising insight into what mobile technologies will look like over the next five years

The future of mobile communications was foreseen in the early 1990s by computer company Sun Microsystems, which adopted the slogan, 'The network is the computer'. This meant that we would quickly replace bloated, over-specified personal computers with slimline, portable devices, which were dubbed at the time 'thin clients'.

This turned out to be a false dawn, for at the time wireline telecommunications services for voice and data were hopelessly ill-equipped to deliver on the promise of network computing even for fixed devices, let alone mobile ones. Reliability was poor, while coverage was patchy, leaving branch offices and remote locations starved of bandwidth.

EXECUTIVE SUMMARY

○ the era of network computing will arrive in the next five years

○ 4G will deliver key benefits, such as a seamless global office, better management of assets, location- and 'presence'-based services and cost reductions

○ any disparity in cost or bandwidth between fixed and mobile access will disappear

○ other technologies, such as the long-range WiMAX, and short-range Bluetooth and RFID, will complement 3G/4G networks

network computing: a reality

But now network computing is becoming a reality, and over the next five years will transform the working landscape, for SMEs in particular. Until now the most advanced mobile communications services have been mostly within the reach of large enterprise IT departments, while SMEs have lagged a year or two behind. Going forward, mobile services are set to democratise communications, presenting company and home workers – and road warriors – with access to all the bandwidth they need, coupled with sophisticated tracking and location-based facilities.

Indeed the next revolution in mobile communications will bring SMEs four key benefits under the banner of 4G (fourth generation mobile) and fixed/mobile convergence (the blend of fixed-line and mobile communications):

- a seamless global office, enjoying equal access from everywhere to any system or device. Users will be able to access their full desktop, email, and diary from anywhere, either from a laptop or mobile handset

- ability to manage assets, including people, equipment, vehicles and products, far more effectively. Location tracking will enable all these resources to be pinpointed, and deployed more effectively

- a range of innovative new services based on location and mobility. These will include 'presence' applications that support mobile collaborative working, and videoconferencing

- consolidation and significant reduction in the overall cost of communications, combining voice and data, wherever the source and destination, into a single predictable service and bill

increased bandwidth and lower costs

The two main factors underpinning these benefits are the rapid increase in bandwidth, and reduction in cost for mobile data services. This process is not yet complete, but within five years any disparity in cost or bandwidth between fixed and mobile access will have vanished, within the UK and much of Europe. As a result, mobile access will predominate, with fixed lines often relegated to so-called 'backhauling' duties – sending traffic back to the network operator. In business premises or homes, this will happen via the usual DSL or cable broadband networks, or better still by optical fibre, which will also offer all manner of fast interactive services. The point is that the devices themselves – even PCs and server computers – need no longer be plugged directly into the fixed lines.

a decline for Wi-Fi?

More controversially perhaps, mobile operators such as Vodafone are predicting that emerging 4G services will take over from the short-range Wi-Fi technology used in 'hotspots', such as train stations and in the home and office. They claim Wi-Fi will become redundant for several reasons. One factor is the wide coverage of mobile networks. Another is Wi-Fi's potentially weaker security in public places, while over mobile networks access can only be gained from a device with the right SIM card, adding an additional protection factor. Further, 4G services will match or exceed the data speeds available over Wi-Fi. Meanwhile, in businesses and homes people will be able to deploy their own wireless access points for mobile phones – called femtocells and picocells – which are like scaled-down versions of the large mobile phone base stations deployed by network operators.

There is also another emerging technology called WiMAX. This is a longer range technology than Wi-Fi and is being deployed by some mobile operators as a high-speed service to complement 3G/4G systems, depending on spectrum availability.

Current 3G data services that are already widely deployed in most developed countries allow access at an effective average speed of around one megabit per second, which is a realistic measure. This is about the same as the latest Wi-Fi and, for that matter, much broadband fixed-line internet access over DSL on ordinary telephone lines. It is quite adequate for web surfing, email, voice and file download. With 4G, which will be rolled out over the next few years, the bit rate could increase to a peak of 100 megabits per second, which is more than sufficient for a host of emerging multimedia applications and also high definition, mobile TV.

affordability of new services

Equally important is that mobile data services at this speed will be available at an affordable fixed rate. This will enable an SME to budget effectively for all its communication needs, giving staff whatever capacity they need wherever they are.

Costs cannot be predicted exactly, but it could be an 'all you can eat' for, say, £50 a month for each employee. And the ways to get online to mobile broadband will evolve. Notebook computers will be shipped with internal capability to access 3G/4G networks, in the same way they now access Wi-Fi.

The combination of location and bandwidth will introduce 'presence' into mobile services, bringing the possibility, for example, of staging ad hoc teleconferences among people on the move, without the need of a videoconferencing suite. The quality will actually be far better than is possible at present with videoconferencing over the internet, via services such as Skype. In addition, it will be feasible to stream high-definition video from a mobile handset, which will increasingly be the device that captures pictures of breaking news events.

The speed and flexibility of field worker applications will also increase greatly, as workers such as healthcare professionals and salespeople gain access to rich interaction with content, such as patient and customer data. Unifying services, such as instant messaging and satellite location, will enable the right people to be contacted at the right time.

fast set-up and targeting

Another significant point is that when high mobile data rates are universally available, new applications become possible, even when these involve fixed equipment. The key here is that given mobile access, new equipment can be brought online almost instantly, without the delay or cost of deployment involved in running a fixed-line to a given location. For example, digital advertising screens can be deployed temporarily for large public events. This brings us to another important capability – the ability to identify mobile phone users on location, which makes it possible, in principle, to select adverts according to the interests of people who happen to be in the vicinity.

Indeed, the combination of consistent high bandwidth and mobility will be a potent one, facilitating many applications over the next few years that have been held back by cost and time restrictions on deployment. Some of the potential applications will be controversial, with implications for privacy. The ability to set up surveillance cameras quickly, or the potential to track movements of staff, or even the general public, come into this category. This may not be such an issue for SMEs, since tracking staff in the context of their work is unlikely to be controversial, and probably executed on the basis of an opt-in that can be turned off. After all, commercial vehicle movements have been tracked for years.

Bluetooth

All these applications exploit mobile access to global networks, but there will also be exciting developments in the field of local communications among devices in very close proximity. The Bluetooth wireless system widely used in mobile phones can be used now to synchronise handsets with PCs for email. Now the potential exists for extending this to create local networks comprising devices that happen to be close by at the time. This could be used, for example, for distributing information locally among large numbers of people at a major sporting or entertainment event, rather than having to clog up access bandwidth by sending the information separately to every mobile.

Radio Frequency IDentification

At even shorter range, RFID (Radio Frequency IDentification) is set to proliferate as current trials consolidate into commercial deployments. At present, most of the trial applications are concerned with theft prevention, inventory management or electronic payment, and applicable only to larger enterprises. Tesco, for example, is tagging shopping baskets to tackle 'walk out theft'. In the next few years, as the technology becomes more mature and widely available in mobile devices, its appeal to smaller companies will grow. Allowing employees' mobiles to be used in place of smart cards for controlling access to offices is just one example of the potential benefits.

RFID can also be used to replace bar code reading whenever this brings an advantage. The main advantage is that an RFID-tagged device does not wait to be scanned, since it is transmitting signals all the time, and so has the potential for automated, and error-free, stock taking, for example. Nonetheless, it does have some disadvantages at present, such as cost of deployment and range. But as these are resolved, the technology will bring about a growing number of applications involving local tracking or recognition.

The broad message is that the era of network computing will truly arrive over the next five years, and this time we really can dispense with our 'fat' devices, perhaps even including laptops, with impunity. Indeed, one irony of the mobile communications revolution may be that we will no longer need a mobile device for computation, since this will be done by servers within the network. This will happen either in-house or, more likely for SMEs, by companies such as Salesforce.com, which is now promoting a wholesale move to applications shared by many, and hosted remotely on its own systems.

Even those people needing a keyboard and screen while on the move may well find these conveniently located with fast mobile internet connections wherever they happen to be, as these will become low-cost commodity devices.

SUMMARY – COMING SOON TO THE MOBILE WORLD

High-speed broadband coupled with even better geographical coverage and further device innovation will take mobile communications forward on several fronts over the next five years, including:

- ☐ 4G will bring true mobile broadband – the advent of 4G services over the next few years will deliver real speeds of 10 Mbps, matching or exceeding Wi-Fi, while retaining the advantages of privacy brought by the SIM card. With 4G also offering full roaming and even better coverage than 3G, Wi-Fi could become history

- ☐ SIM ID – the globally unique number for each SIM card will deliver true network computing. The dream of real network computing delivering consistent service to any device will at last become reality. It will no longer be necessary to lug a heavy laptop around to have full access to your applications and data – these will now be able to reside on a server with much greater protection against loss. All that will be needed will be a mobile handset, or screen and keyboard where needed, which will still be much lighter than a laptop, and consume less than half as much power

- ☐ remote asset management – use of mobile tags and other devices will allow you to manage your assets from any point, wherever they happen to be. Assets can include equipment, products and employees, tracking all of which can reduce costs and improve service

- ☐ digital signage – flexible low-power plastic displays will be used for dynamic advertising, and no longer confined to locations with fixed-line access to a network. They can be instantly connected to a mobile network, which can also be exploited for 'smart advertising', taking account of known preferences of people within the area, identified by their mobile handset

3G.co.uk
Third generation mobile news and information
www.3g.co.uk

Business Link
Government business advice
www.businesslink.gov.uk

Choose Another Way
Scottish government site on sustainable transport and working
www.chooseanotherway.com

Content Futures
News site on mobile content
www.contentfutures.com

Employers and work-life balance
www.employersforwork-lifebalance.org.uk

Flexibility
New ways of working site
www.flexibility.co.uk

Gartner
IT/telecoms analyst
www.gartner.com

GSM Association
Global mobile industry body
www.gsmworld.com

Henley Management Centre – Future Work Forum
Research on future work
www.henleymc.ac.uk/fwf

Homeworking.com

UK homeworking resource site

www.homeworking.com

Jupiter Research

Analyst focusing on the internet and consumer technology

www.jupiterresearch.com

Microsoft

Technology advice for SMEs

www.microsoft.com/uk/smallbusiness

Mobile Computer Users Group

www.mcug.org.uk

Mobile Data Association

Promotes the uses and benefits of mobile data

www.themda.org

Mobileinfo

Mobile and wireless site

www.mobileinfo.com

Mobile Marketing Association UK

UK chapter of a global body

www.mmaglobal.com/uk

National Computing Centre

Largest corporate membership body in the UK IT sector

www.ncc.co.uk

Nomad
Centre of excellence for mobile and flexible working in local government
www.projectnomad.org.uk

Ofcom
Communications regulator
www.ofcom.org.uk

Quocirca
IT analyst specialising in business impact
www.quocirca.com

Ovum
IT/telecoms analyst
www.ovum.com

Society of Information Technology Management
Professional association for ICT managers working in and for the
public sector
www.socitm.gov.uk

Telework Association
Membership organisation providing information, advice and support to
enable individuals, whether employed or self employed, to make a success
of mobile, home-based and flexible ways of working
www.tca.org.uk

TUC
Work-life balance from the union perspective
www.tuc.org.uk/changingtimes

Unified Communications Expo
Site of annual UK show
www.unifiedcommsexpo.com

Vodafone
Details of mobile applications
www.vodafonebusiness.co.uk/applications

Vodafone Working Nation
Examining social drivers underpinning developments in technology
www.vodafone.com/working_nation.html

Voice over IP news site
www.voip-news.com

Voice over IP resources
www.voip.org.uk

Work Foundation
Working life research
www.theworkfoundation.com

Work Wise UK
Smarter working campaign
www.workwiseuk.org

Yankee Group
Analyst specialising in connectivity
www.yankeegroup.com